The Start-Up Guide for Tech Innovators

Tech Innovators

Launching Your Tech Company

Introduction

Welcome to "The Start-Up Guide for Tech Innovators: Launching Your Tech Company." In today's fast-paced and ever-evolving world, technology is at the forefront of innovation and disruption. As a tech innovator, you have the power to shape the future, revolutionize industries, and create a lasting impact.

Launching a tech company can be an exhilarating yet daunting journey. There are countless decisions to be made, hurdles to overcome, and risks to navigate. However, with the right knowledge, strategies, and mindset, you can transform your vision into a thriving and successful venture.

This guide is designed to be your compass as you navigate the entrepreneurial landscape. It will provide you with a comprehensive roadmap, encompassing everything from ideation to execution, funding to product development, branding to scaling, and much more. Each chapter is carefully crafted to equip you with the necessary tools and insights to make informed decisions, avoid common pitfalls, and position your tech company for success.

But launching a tech company is not just about business strategies and financial gains. It's about pursuing a dream, making a difference, and leaving a mark on the world. It's about embracing challenges, learning from failures, and constantly pushing the boundaries of what is possible. This guide will not only help you build a successful tech company but also inspire you to become a true tech innovator.

So, if you are ready to embark on this exciting journey and turn your tech dreams into reality, let's dive in. Together, we will unlock the secrets, navigate the complexities, and unleash the potential of your tech company. Get ready to disrupt, revolutionize, and make your mark in the ever-evolving world of technology. The future awaits, and you are about to embark on an extraordinary adventure.

Chapter One

Introduction to Tech Innovators Business

1.1 The Importance of Tech Innovation in the Business World

In today's digitally-driven era, technology innovation plays a pivotal role in shaping the landscape of the business world. From small startups to multinational corporations, businesses across all industries are recognizing the immense benefits and potential that tech innovation brings. It has become a critical factor in determining a company's competitiveness, growth potential, and long-term sustainability.

1. Enhancing Efficiency and Productivity

   One of the key advantages of tech innovation in the business world is its ability to enhance efficiency and productivity. Through the utilization of automation, advanced software solutions, and artificial intelligence, companies can streamline their processes, reduce manual errors, and optimize resource allocation. This leads to significant time and cost savings, allowing businesses to operate more effectively and allocate their resources towards more value-added tasks.

2. Driving Customer Centricity and Experience

   Tech innovation also plays a crucial role in driving customer centricity and enhancing the overall customer experience. Companies today are leveraging technologies such as data analytics, machine learning, and customer relationship management (CRM) systems to gain valuable insights into customer behaviour, preferences, and needs. By understanding these insights, businesses can tailor their products, services, and marketing strategies to meet the evolving demands of their target audience. Consequently, this leads to increased customer satisfaction, loyalty, and ultimately, business growth.

3. Fostering Innovation and Differentiation

Innovation is the lifeblood of any successful business. By embracing tech innovation, companies can foster a culture of creativity, experimentation, and continuous improvement. With the advent of emerging technologies like blockchain, the Internet of Things (IoT), and augmented reality (AR), businesses have access to exciting new possibilities to revolutionize their products, services, and operations. Leveraging these technologies allows companies to differentiate themselves from competitors, enter new markets, and gain a competitive edge in an increasingly crowded marketplace.

4. Unlocking New Business Opportunities

Tech innovation has the power to unlock new business opportunities and disrupt traditional industries. Startups and entrepreneurs who leverage technology to identify unmet needs and industry gaps can create innovative solutions and carve out new niches in the market. By identifying and capitalizing on emerging trends, technologies, and consumer demands, businesses can pioneer new business models, expand their revenue streams, and gain a significant market advantage.

5. Enabling Global Collaboration and Connectivity

The advancements in communication technology have revolutionized the way businesses collaborate and operate across borders. With cloud computing, video conferencing, and project management tools, teams from different geographical locations can seamlessly work together, share ideas, and execute projects in real time. This level of connectivity and collaboration has broken down barriers, eliminated geographical limitations, and opened up a world of opportunities for businesses to thrive in a globalized economy.

6. Driving Economic Growth and Job Creation

Lastly, tech innovation is a catalyst for economic growth and job creation. According to studies, tech-driven industries have consistently outperformed other sectors in terms of job creation, making them an essential driver of economic prosperity. As businesses embrace tech innovation, they create new roles, foster entrepreneurship, and contribute to economic development. Moreover, the advancements in technology often lead to the creation of entirely new industries, further expanding the job market and fostering economic growth.

1.2 What it takes to be a successful tech innovator

Embarking on a journey to become a successful tech innovator requires a blend of inherent abilities, learned skills, cultivated traits, and unwavering determination. The world of tech innovation is rewarding, albeit challenging. It can provide an opportunity to revolutionize industries, solve societal problems, and shape the future. However, it requires more than just a ground-breaking idea or a mastery of technology.

1. Impeccable Technological Acumen

   Firstly and most obviously, a successful tech innovator must possess a deep understanding and mastery of technology. Being well-versed in the latest technologies, staying abreast of emerging trends, and constantly enhancing tech competencies is of utmost importance. This understanding enables innovators to know what's technologically feasible, what's coming next, and how these advancements can be leveraged to create value.

2. Creative Problem-Solving Abilities

   Successful tech innovators are essentially problem solvers. They have the ability to identify gaps, conceptualize creative solutions, and iterate the ideas to effectively solve unique challenges. They apply a design thinking approach by emphasizing empathy, encouraging ideation, advocating prototyping, and embracing failures. Their innovative solutions often challenge the status quo and push the boundaries of what's possible.

3. Risk-taking and Resilience

Perseverance and resilience are integral attributes of successful tech innovators. The path of innovation is riddled with uncertainties, risks, and failures. Innovators often face scepticism, setbacks, and challenges that can be demotivating and pushing them off course. Being resilient allows innovators to maintain their course in the face of adversity, pick themselves up after failures, learn from their mistakes, and keep trying until they succeed.

4. Astute Business Acumen

It's essential to possess a keen understanding of business fundamentals. This understanding enables innovators to create viable business models, develop effective marketing strategies, manage financials, and understand the subtleties of legal, regulatory, and intellectual property issues. Successful tech innovators understand that innovation is not just about creating novel technologies, but also involves successfully commercializing these technologies in a manner that delivers value to the customers and stakeholders.

5. Exceptional Communication and Leadership Skills

Tech innovators often need to inspire, lead, persuade, and negotiate. They need to effectively communicate the potential of their ideas to their teams, investors, partners, and customers. Good leadership skills are vital for rallying the team, articulating vision, fostering collaboration, and driving the project towards success.

6. Ethical Responsibility

   Finally, successful tech innovators are conscious of their ethical responsibilities. They understand the potential impacts of their innovations and work to ensure that they bring positive change to society. They consider privacy, security, and societal implications, and they strive to foster trust and transparency.

1.3 Overview of the start-up journey

Embarking on a start-up journey can be an exhilarating and challenging adventure filled with highs and lows. It is often said that to navigate these tumultuous waters, one needs to understand the map. In essence, the start-up journey describes the key stages that a start-up embarks on, from inception to scale. For those who dare to take this route, this section provides a high-level overview of that exciting journey.

Idea Inception

The journey begins with an idea. It is the spark that fuels innovation - an observation of a gap in the market, a pain point yet to be addressed or simply, a unique solution to an existing problem. In this stage, founders refine their idea and validate its potential in the market. Is there a need? Is the timing right? Is the solution feasible?

Business Planning

Once the idea is refined, it's time to create a business plan. This document is a crucial roadmap, detailing the business' vision, mission, market potential, revenue model, competitive landscape, marketing strategies, and financial projections. The business plan serves as a strategic guide for the start-up and a persuasive document to potential investors and stakeholders.

Team Building

No start-up can succeed without a capable and dedicated team. In the team-building phase, founders assemble individuals with complementary skill sets. This dynamic team, composed of motivated and talented individuals, work together towards the common mission and vision of the start-up.

Prototype Development

In the prototype development stage, the start-up begins translating the idea into a tangible product or service. They design and develop a prototype, subsequently iterating and refining it based on feedback and testing. This stage is critical for demonstrating the viability of the product and receiving early feedback from potential users.

Securing Funding

Once the prototype is in place, the start-up often requires capital to move to the next level - entering the market. Thus, the fundraising phase begins. Start-ups can secure funding from various sources, such as angel investors, venture capitalists, government grants, or crowdfunding platforms. The fund-raising process often involves pitching the business idea, negotiating terms, and romancing potential investors.

Product Launch

After securing funding, the start-up moves towards launching the product in the marketplace. This involves extensive marketing and sales efforts to create awareness, attract customers, and drive sales. Furthermore, listening to customer feedback at this stage is imperative to refine and improve the product.

Scaling Up

In the scaling phase, start-ups strive to grow their operations, reach, and profits at an exponential rate. This involves expanding to new markets, diversifying product offerings, optimizing operations, and strengthening the brand presence. The primary challenge in the scaling phase is to manage fast-paced growth while maintaining product quality and customer satisfaction.

Exit Strategy

Finally, start-ups need to have an exit strategy in place. An exit can take several forms - it can be an acquisition by a larger company, a merger with another company, or going public through an Initial Public Offering (IPO). The exit strategy should align with the company's long-term goals and provide substantial returns for its stakeholders.

Chapter Two

Identifying a Problem and Finding a Solution

2.1 Conducting market research

In the realm of tech innovation, the success of a startup is often predicated on the ability to identify a problem and devise a solution that's not just technologically feasible but also aligns with market needs. Market research is a systematic process that can enable tech innovators to reach these actionable insights. It informs decision-making, reduces risk, and lays the foundation for a viable and scalable business model.

Understanding the Importance of Market Research

Before diving into the practical steps, it's essential to understand the value of market research for tech innovators. Comprehensive market research can provide clarity on the competitive landscape, emerging trends, and customer behaviours. It helps to identify gaps or inefficiencies in the market, paving the way for innovative solutions. Moreover, it facilitates an understanding of the target audience, guiding the development of a product that fits their needs and preferences.

Conducting Market Research: The Process

1. Define the Objective

The first step in the process is to define clearly the objective of the market research. Is it to identify a problem? Validate an idea? Understand customer behaviour? Depending on the goal, the methods and data required may differ.

2. Identify Your Target Market

The next step is to identify the target market or audience. This involves determining the customer demographics, such as age, location, income, lifestyle, and behavioural traits. A well-defined target market can guide the research process and ensure its relevance and applicability.

3. Choose Your Research Methods

There are two primary types of research - Primary and Secondary. Primary research involves firsthand information collected directly from consumers or competitors, through surveys, interviews, or observations. Secondary research, on the other hand, involves analyzing data already collected and published by others, such as industry reports, articles, or databases. Usually, a combination of both methods is utilized.

4. Collect and Analyze the Data

Next, gather the necessary data using the chosen research methods. Depending on the scope and scale of the research, this could be a time-intensive process. After the data is collected, it's time for analysis. The data should be reviewed to identify patterns, trends, and insights. It's essential to approach this stage objectively to yield unbiased and useful results.

5. Generate Insights and Make Decisions

The final step is to interpret the findings and use them to guide decision-making. These insights may confirm an initial hypothesis, uncover a new problem, or indicate a market demand. Whatever the findings, they should inform the next steps, whether it's tweaking an idea, pivoting the target market, or even reshaping the entire concept.

2.2 Identifying pain points and gaps in the market

The journey of a tech innovator is often paved with problems, challenges, and uncertainties. One key to overcoming these hurdles is being able to identify the pain points of the market and the gaps within that market. The process of identifying these issues and creating effective solutions evolves the startup from a mere idea to a tangible and successful business model.

Understanding Pain Points

Pain points refer to the problems and challenges faced by potential customers in the market. They are essentially the underlying factors that prompt the need for a solution, a problem needing to be solved. Identifying pain points helps tech innovators to realize the precise needs of their customers and tailor their solutions accordingly.

Recognizing Gaps in The Market

A market gap is essentially an unmet customer need or an underserved customer segment in the market. Identifying these gaps provides tech innovators with the opportunity to step in with a unique solution. This process involves extensive market research and understanding the segment better to address the unmet needs.

Steps to Identify Pain Points and Market Gaps

1. Identify Your Target Market: Identify and understand your target market. This includes understanding their demographics, needs, wants, and challenges.

2. Customer Interaction and Feedback: Engage with the customers and get feedback. Interactions can be either in the form of one-on-one interviews or through surveys.

3. Observe the Trends: Keep track of market trends and customer behavior. This includes keeping an

eye on social media trends and understanding what is popular or desired.

4. Competitor Analysis: Identify what your competitors are offering and where they lack. This could provide the perfect opportunity to step in and fill in the gaps.

5. Continuous Learning and Evolving: Finally, it's about continuous learning. Market trends, customer needs and technology are constantly evolving. A one-time identification process is not enough. Continuous learning will enable you to adapt your solution to an ever-changing market scenario.

2.3 Developing a unique value proposition

Once pain points and market gaps are identified, the next progressive step is to formulate a unique solution that would alleviate these issues. This calls for the creation of a unique value proposition (UVP) that would distinguish the startup from the rest. The UVP becomes a beacon of differentiation and a powerful driver of competitive advantage in the market.

Understanding the Unique Value Proposition

The Unique Value Proposition (UVP) is a clear, concise, and compelling statement that outlines how your startup's solution is different from and superior to others. It highlights the unique way your tech startup addresses customer problems and fills market gaps. UVP demonstrates the value, relevance, and intrigue of your solution.

Crafting a Strong Unique Value Proposition

Creating a strong value proposition involves understanding your customer, your product, and the market dynamics. Here is a step-by-step guide:

1. Understand Your Customer: Begin by analyzing who your target customers are. Understand their needs, lifestyles, psychographics, and the problems they are seeking to solve.

2.

3. Evaluate Your Solution: Next, take a deep dive into your solution. Define its features, advantages, and how it meets customer needs. Answer the question, 'What value does this provide to my customers?'

4. Understand Your Competition: Assess the existing competitors in your market and understand their offer. Identify their value propositions, strengths, and areas where they fall short.

5. Differentiation: Identify what sets you apart from the competition. This includes identifying key differentiators like technology leveraged, pricing model, customer service, design, etc. This becomes the crux of your UVP.

After gathering these insights, create a succinct statement that encapsulates the unique value that your solution provides for the customers. The stronger and clearer your UVP, the better the chances for your solution to stand out amidst stiff competition.

Examples of Strong Unique Value Propositions

- Slack- "Be less busy"- Slack offers a solution that reduces work and resultantly, reduces stress for the user.

- Unbounce - "A/B testing without tech headaches"- Unbounce removes a major pain point of technicalities in conducting A/B tests.

Chapter Three

Building a Team

3.1 Identifying Key Roles and Skill Sets Needed

Building a winning startup team is crucial to the success of any tech-driven venture. Assembling skilled individuals with distinct skill sets and complementary abilities will ensure the multifaceted challenges of running a successful startup are met effectively. This involves identifying key roles and skills required within the organization and aligning them with the team members.

Key Roles for a Tech Startup

Here are some critical roles to have on your tech startup team that can drive you toward success:

1. Founder or Co-Founder(s): Visionary leaders who conceptualize the venture, articulate the mission, define the company culture, and spearhead its evolution.

2. Product Manager: A product expert responsible for defining product requirements, prioritizing features, managing timelines and ensuring the product aligns with the overall strategy.

3. Software Developers/Engineers: This technical team is responsible for coding and developing the core technology, ensuring the smooth and efficient functioning of the solution offered.

4. UI/UX Designer: Responsible for creating an intuitive and visually appealing user experience for the product or solution catering to customer needs and expectations.

5. Sales and Marketing Specialists: This team focuses on creating brand awareness, driving customer

acquisition and generating revenue for the startup. They formulate marketing strategies, manage public relations, and develop growth hack initiatives.

6. Customer Support and Success Manager: The backbone of customer retention and satisfaction, this individual takes ownership of customer relationship management and works to ensure customer satisfaction and issue resolution.

7. Human Resource (HR) Manager: A crucial role in team management, the HR manager is responsible for hiring, team-building, managing employee benefits, and ensuring smooth onboarding of new hires.

8. Operations Manager: Ensures seamless day-to-day functioning of the startup, overseeing project timelines and milestones, resource allocation, and process improvement.

9. Finance Manager/Controller: This role manages the venture's finances, budgeting, forecasting, and financial planning. They ensure financial compliance and monitor the startup's cash flow.

Essential Skills for Startup Success

In addition to the roles, identifying the right skill set for team members is crucial. Some essential skills to look for in the team members are:

1. Problem Solving: Tech startups are bound to face challenges that require innovative thinking and creative problem-solving.

2. Adaptability: Startup ventures grow and change rapidly. Prospective team members should be adaptable and willing to tackle new challenges with agility and enthusiasm.

3. Critical Thinking: Decision-making should be driven by logical analysis and evaluation, a critical thinking

skill that allows startups to keep up with industry trends and maintain a competitive edge.

4. Communication: In a fast-paced, collaborative environment, a startup team needs to share and convey ideas effectively, both internally and with customers, investors, and other stakeholders.

5. Customer-centricity: Aligning the organization's mission, culture, and product in sync with customer needs is crucial for success. The ability to empathize with customers and embrace their feedback is an essential skill.

3.2 Hiring and onboarding process

Once the necessary roles and skill sets have been identified, the next step in building a team for a tech startup is to establish a thorough and efficient hiring and onboarding process. A solid structure at this stage ensures the best talent is brought on board and sets a positive precedent for new employees, aiding in the retention of these hires.

Hiring Process: Steps for Successful Recruitment

Identifying the Need: Begin by accurately defining the roles and skills your startup needs. This includes creating clear job descriptions and outlining the qualifications, skills and experience required.

1. Sourcing Candidates: Use various resources such as professional networking sites, job portals, college job fairs, and employee referrals. Use targeted job postings to effectively reach potential candidates.

2. Screening and Shortlisting: Review resumes meticulously and select the ones that meet the

criteria you've outlined. Screening calls can be used as an initial step to filter applicants.

3. Interviewing: This step involves interviewing the shortlisted candidates. The interview should assess both technical skills and soft skills. Consider including practical assignments or tests, particularly for technical roles.

4. Reference Checks & Background Verification: Make sure to verify details provided by the candidates. Contact references from previous employers or colleagues and perform background checks for further validation.

5. Making an Offer: After the decision is made, extend an official offer to the candidate. This should include the remuneration details, job role, and other terms of employment.

Onboarding Process: Integrating New Team Members

1. Pre-Onboarding Communication: Establish contact with new employees before their official start date. Send them the necessary documents, equipment, and other details to make their 'first day' smooth and hassle-free.

2. Orientation: Introduce the new hires to the organization, its objectives, culture, and workplace environment. Provide them with an overview of the organizational structure and their respective teams.

3. Job-specific Training: Provide in-depth, comprehensive training that will help new hires understand their jobs better. This includes understanding the product, processes, methods, and tools they will be using.

4. Mentoring and Evaluation: Assign a mentor or buddy for the new hire. Regularly evaluate their performance and provide feedback.

5. Integration into Culture: Lastly, make new hires feel part of the team. Include them in team meetings, company gatherings, and social events. Make sure they feel valued and part of the startup community from day one.

3.3 Building a cohesive and talented team

Building a team is indeed a vital activity for any tech startup. However, there's more to it than simply gathering individuals with matching skill sets and qualifications. For a tech startup to thrive, it's equally important to construct a cohesive and talented team. Weaving together individuals into a unified entity not only enhances productivity but also cultivates a shared sense of purpose and vision.

Identifying Talent

Identifying talent is the initial and significant step in building a great team. When the right talents come together, they function as a competent team, with the ability to drive the startup towards its goals.

- Spot the Potential: Look out for qualities like versatility, creativity, relentless problem-solving capability and the willingness to learn and adapt.

- Diversity is Key: Garnering a team with diverse backgrounds can bring in a range of perspectives, thereby fostering innovative thinking and creative solutions.

- Skills and Experience Matter: If you want your tech startup to hit the ground running, having a good mix of fresh and experienced talents is necessary. Senior team members usually provide stability, while junior members bring fresh perspectives and trending skill sets.

Building Cohesion

Cohesion is the glue that binds your talented team together. It flourishes when team members align themselves with shared goals and values, enhancing their capacity to function seamlessly as a single unit thereby accelerating the pace of growth.

- Cultivate Trust: The foundation of a great team lies in trust. A team that trusts each other can function without unnecessary bottlenecks like bureaucracy or micromanagement.

- Open Communication: To safeguard the health of a team, it's crucial to establish a culture of open communication where every team member feels heard and valued.

- Conflict Management: Conflicts are inevitable in a team. However, with the right conflict management strategies in place, these hurdles can be converted into stepping stones for growth and learning.

Fostering Culture

Culture is what differentiates a group of people from a team. Cultivating a shared culture nurtures a shared identity and paves the way for synergy.

- Diversity and Inclusion: Successful teams are those that celebrate their diversity and create an inclusive atmosphere where everyone feels they belong.

- Team Building Activities: Regular team building activities can help to break the ice and foster a sense of camaraderie among team members.

- Continuous Learning: Establishing a culture of continuous learning can lead to constant improvement and innovation. This keeps the team's skills up to date and sustains the intensity of their performance.

Chapter Four

Developing a Business Plan

4.1 Defining Business Objectives and Goals

Behind every successful tech startup lies a clear and structured business plan, which essentially serves as the compass guiding the organization towards its ultimate vision. Critical to the formulation of this blueprint is the definition of business objectives and goals. This process helps in setting the framework for the journey ahead and aids in the development of precise strategies to accomplish these targets.

Defining Business Objectives

Objectives provide a high-level view of what your business wants to achieve. They define the direction of the business and need to be aligned with the business's vision and purpose.

- Understand Your Vision: Recognize what you want your startup to achieve in the long run. Is it to be a leader in the tech space, provide the best user experience, or disrupt the industry with pathbreaking innovations? Your vision becomes the cornerstone for setting your business objectives.

- Advocate SMART Objectives: Ensure your objectives are Specific, Measurable, Achievable, Relevant, and Time-based (SMART). This approach ensures clarity and precision, propelling your business in the right direction.

- Diversify Your Objectives: Your objectives should cover various areas of the business, including financial stability, customer satisfaction, market presence, talent acquisition, and product development, to ensure holistic growth.

Formulating Goals

With the business objectives in place, the next step involves defining the goals, which represent the tangible steps taken to realize the objectives. Here's how you can set effective goals:

- Prioritize High-Impact Goals: In the early stages of a tech startup, resources are limited, and every effort must count. Focus on achieving goals that align with your objectives and have the potential to make a significant impact.

- Quantify Your Goals: Goals need to be quantifiable and time-bound for effective tracking and measurement. For instance, aim to achieve "15%

growth in user base by the end of Quarter 3" or "reduce product development cycle time by 20% in six months."

- Establish Clear Accountability: Each goal must have a clear owner who takes the responsibility for its completion. Clear accountability promotes ownership and facilitates systematic progress tracking.

Integrating Into the Business Plan

Integrating these objectives and goals into your business plan is the final step. They need to serve as the foundation of your strategic planning and decision-making process.

- Inclusion in the Executive Summary: Your objectives and goals must be clearly communicated in the executive summary of the business plan. This section provides a snapshot of your intentions and highlights the direction in which the company is heading.

- Relating Business Strategies: Connect your objectives and goals with the key strategies laid out in the business plan, creating a linkage that justifies your proposed course of action.

- Use in Monitoring Progress: Utilize your clearly defined objectives and goals as performance benchmarks. Regular assessment against these parameters will provide a reality check on your startup's progress and achievements.

4.2 Crafting a mission statement

The mission statement of a tech startup is comparable to its DNA - a fundamental building block that captures the essence of its existence. A well-crafted mission statement defines a startup's purpose, reveals its intention, and outlines its approach to reach its goals. It plays a monumental role in developing a strategic and effective business plan.

Understanding the Importance of a Mission Statement

As a tech innovator, acknowledging the importance of a mission statement is the first step towards crafting it.

- Defines Purpose: A mission statement articulates the purpose of your startup, providing answers to why it exists and what it hopes to achieve.

- Guides Strategic Decisions: It shapes the strategies and influences key decisions, acting as a guiding light during the startup's growth and development stages.

- Aligns Team: When everyone in the organization understands the startup's mission, it unites them under a common purpose, fostering cohesion and productivity.

Crafting the Mission Statement

The process of crafting a mission statement requires clarity, vision, and an understanding of your startup's nucleus.

- Identify Core Values: What does your organization firmly believe in? Innovation, customer satisfaction, sustainability? These core values serve as the backbone of your mission statement.

- Define Core Purpose: Why does your startup exist? To solve a specific problem, to meet a market need, or to change the tech landscape? This question helps you articulate your organization's core purpose.

- Illustrate Core Strategy: How will your startup make its vision a reality? Your approach to achieving your goals forms the final element of your mission statement.

Integrating the Mission Statement into the Business Plan

Once you've formulated a potent mission statement, it's time to properly weave it into your business plan.

1. Include in the Executive Summary: Incorporate the mission statement in the executive summary of your business plan. This gives stakeholders an immediate understanding of your startup's purpose.

2. Connect with Business Objectives: Align your mission statement with your business objectives. This connection helps stakeholders see how your startup's mission contributes to the realization of its objectives.

3. Relate to Operational & Marketing Strategies: Your operation and marketing strategies should reflect your mission statement. This highlights how your startup's activities align with its mission.

Real-World Examples of Powerful Mission Statements

Let's look at some powerful mission statements from tech giants for inspiration:

- Google: "To organize the world's information and make it universally accessible and useful."

- Microsoft: "To empower every person and every organization on the planet to achieve more."

- These mission statements are clear, concise, and communicate the startups' purpose, values, and strategies effectively.

4.3 Conducting a SWOT analysis

A SWOT (Strengths, Weaknesses, Opportunities, and Threats) analysis is a valuable component of any business plan, helping startups identify their current status and future potential. For tech innovators, a comprehensive

SWOT analysis not only unveils crucial insights that can shape the startup's growth trajectory but also signifies a well-structured and carefully contemplated business plan.

Understanding the Importance of a SWOT Analysis

The significance of a SWOT analysis extends across the organization, providing a holistic view of the internal and external environment in which the tech startup operates.

- Informs Business Strategy: A SWOT analysis helps build robust business strategies, ensuring any strategy selected takes into consideration the startup's specific circumstances.

- Uncovers Opportunities and Threats: It shines a light on emerging market opportunities and potential threats, enabling tech startups to take preemptive action and capitalize on prospects.

- Delivers a Competitive Advantage: Analyzing the startup's strengths and weaknesses as compared to the competition offers insights into the competitive landscape and contributes to carving out a distinct market position.

Conducting the SWOT Analysis

To execute a comprehensive SWOT analysis, startups must dissect each of the four components in the context of their individual businesses.

1. Strengths

Identify what your tech startup does better than its competitors, which in-house resources provide an advantage, and what unique selling propositions (USPs) stand out.

- Expertise in specialized technologies
- A diverse and skilled team

Intellectual property or proprietary products

2. Weaknesses

Discover areas of improvement for your startup. These may include elements that hinder your potential or result in a competitive disadvantage.

- Limited financial resources
- Insufficient brand recognition
- Dependence on a few clients

3. Opportunities

Investigate the market and industry for new prospects your startup could benefit from. These possibilities often arise from trends, changes, or gaps in the market.

- Emerging technologies to integrate
- Industry expansion or untapped niches
- New collaboration or partnership potential

4. Threats

Uncover potential challenges or risks that could negatively impact your tech startup.

- Rising competition or market saturation

- Regulatory changes or legal concerns
- Economic downturns or unpredictability

Integrating the SWOT Analysis into the Business Plan

Once your SWOT analysis is complete, the next step is to integrate it seamlessly into your business plan.

1. Incorporate in the Market Analysis: Present your SWOT analysis as a part of the market analysis in your business plan. This demonstrates a thorough understanding of your startup's current position and future potential.

2. Align with Business Strategy: Your business strategies should be a reflection of your SWOT analysis. Show how your strategies leverage your strengths and opportunities, and address your weaknesses and threats.

3. Enrich the Marketing Plan: Use the insights from the SWOT analysis to develop a marketing plan that effectively showcases your USPs, promotes brand recognition, and penetrates untapped markets.

4.4 Creating a financial plan and revenue model

A solid financial plan and a sustainable revenue model sit at the heart of every successful tech startup business plan. These elements help encapsulate the financial health, profitability potential, and long-term viability of the startup. They aid in attracting investors, managing finances effectively, and enabling strategic growth-oriented decisions.

Importance of a Financial Plan and Revenue Model

Understanding the need for a financial plan and a revenue model is the preliminary step in this process.

- Facilitates Funding: A well-thought-out financial plan is crucial when securing funding. Investors and financiers demand clear proof of your startup's profitability potential and return on investment (ROI).

- Directs Decision-Making: These financial blueprints act as guiding tools, helping determine strategic business decisions such as pricing, scaling up, resource allocation, and more.

- Ensures Financial Stability: With a sound financial plan and revenue model, startups can effectively manage cash flow, ensuring operational sustainability and paving the way for growth.

Crafting a Financial Plan

The creation of a financial plan entails forecasting three key financial statements: Income Statement (Profit & Loss), Balance Sheet, and Cash Flow Statement.

1. Income Statement

This projection provides an overview of your startup's profitability, highlighting the revenues earned and expenses incurred.

- Revenue Projection: Estimates the revenue your startup is expected to generate over a specific period.
- Expense Forecast: Breaks down projected operational costs, marketing expenses, administrative costs, and other related expenditures.

- Net Profit/Loss: The difference between your revenues and expenses, illustrating whether the startup operates at a profit or loss.

2. Balance Sheet

The balance sheet presents a snapshot of your startup's financial health at a specific point in time, detailing assets, liabilities, and owners' equity.

- Assets: Include your startup's cash, accounts receivables, and other tangible and intangible assets such as property and patents.
- Liabilities: Consist of debts, loans, accounts payable, and other financial obligations.
- Owners' Equity: Reflect the net value of the startup, calculated as assets minus liabilities.

3. Cash Flow Statement

A cash flow statement outlines how cash moves in and out of your startup and is vital for maintaining liquidity.

- Operating Cash Flow: Cash generated from primary business operations.

- Investing Cash Flow: Cash involved in the acquisition or sale of long-term assets.

- Financing Cash Flow: Cash related to funding activities, like loans and equity financing.

Designing a Revenue Model

The next step involves constructing your startup's revenue model, which outlines how the business will generate income.

- Product/Service Sales: Direct income from selling products or services.

- Subscription: Regularly recurring payments for continued access to your product/service.

- Advertisement Revenue: Income from featuring advertisements on your platform.

- Commission: Revenue generated by facilitating transactions between parties.

- Licensing: Allowing others to use your intellectual property in exchange for a fee/license.

Integrating the Financial Plan and Revenue Model into the Business Plan

A well-articulated financial plan and revenue model are vital components of your business plan.

- Include in Financial Section: Clearly detail your financial forecasts and revenue strategy in the business plan's financial section.

- Relate to Business Strategies: Show how your financial and revenue models align with your market analysis, marketing strategy, and overall business objectives.

- Focus on Assumptions: Be transparent about your assumptions. This helps potential investors understand your forecasts and can contribute to financial discussions.

Chapter five

Securing Funding

5.1 Understanding different types of funding options

As a tech entrepreneur, your innovation may be groundbreaking, and your vision unrivalled. But to transform your conceptualised idea into a real-world application, you need to conquer the mountain called "Funding." This is why understanding the different options available to secure this funding is pivotal. Let's explore those various funding types to provide the lifeblood your tech startup requires to succeed.

Personal Investment or Bootstrapping

When getting a startup off the ground, personal investment by far is the simplest and most commonly used method. It includes using personal savings, credit cards, or selling personal assets. One advantage is that you retain total control over your project and don't need to worry about any external pressures or repayments. The caveat is the risk your personal assets bear if your startup fails.

Friends and Family

Another commonly used approach in the early stages is wooing friends and family into investing. They usually require less formal lending structures and can often provide funding quickly without significant red tape. However, it's essential to avoid any unclear agreements to prevent damage to relationships in case of any business failure.

Angel Investors

Angel investors are individuals who provide funding in the startup phase. In return for their investment, they usually require an equity stake in the company. These individuals offer not only financial capital but also their business experience and networks, making them a valuable asset for a tech startup. Entrepreneurs should approach Angel Investors with a strong business plan and market research to reassure them about the investment.

Venture Capitalists (VCs)

Venture Capitalists are firms that professionally manage and invest pooled funds in startups with high growth potential. They typically enter the picture when the startup is past the initial stage and is generating revenues with potential for substantial growth. In return for their significant financial injection, VCs generally demand a say in strategic decisions.

Crowdfunding

In the age of the internet, another popular option is Crowdfunding. This involves raising small amounts of money from a large number of people, typically via the Internet. The draw is that it allows entrepreneurs to retain full control of their company, but success demands a substantial amount of work in promoting the campaign.

Loans and Credit Lines

Traditional bank loans and credit lines are other sources to consider. They come with lower interest rates compared to credit cards but need a solid business plan, good credit history, and often, some collateral.

Government Programs and Grants

Some government organizations offer grants, loans, and financing to support startup technology companies. Each program typically comes with specific qualifications and stipulations, so it's crucial to read the fine print carefully. However, they can be an excellent funding source with potentially fewer strings attached than private funding.

Accelerators and Incubators

Tapping into these resources can provide a great boost for tech startups. Accelerators like Y Combinator or TechStars usually run for a fixed time frame during which businesses get mentorship, office space, and financial resources. In return, they often take a small equity stake in the company.

5.2 Approaching Venture Capitalists and angel investors

Start-ups require substantial investments to turn their innovative ideas into profitable ventures. This investment often comes from venture capitalists and angel investors. However, securing this funding requires a thorough understanding of how to approach and engage these entities. Let's delve into this subject and empower tech innovators with the right knowledge and strategies.

Who are Venture Capitalists and What Do They Offer?

Venture capitalists are individual entities or firms that provide funding to startups predicted to have high growth potential. Usually, venture capitalists (VCs) invest in the latter funding rounds, once the start-up has established the foundational business and has begun to show promise in terms of revenue and growth.

In return for the capital, VCs often ask for equity in the company, allowing them a say in business decisions. Besides finances, VCs also share their extensive business knowledge, strategic expertise, and extensive networks with the start-ups they finance.

Who are Angel Investors and What Do They Offer?

At an even earlier stage - sometimes merely at the idea stage – many startups find financial support in the form of angel investors. These are high-net-worth individuals who finance startups, often in exchange for equity or convertible debt.

Unlike VCs, angel investors use their personal funds and typically invest at an early stage of business when risks are higher. What makes them highly sought after by startups, apart from their willingness to take risks, is their readiness to offer mentorship alongside financial investment.

Differences between Venture Capitalists and Angel Investors

While both venture capitalists and angel investors provide start-ups with the much-needed funding, each comes with its distinction. Angel investors are known for taking bigger risks by investing their own money in the early-stage formation of a company. In contrast, venture capitalists typically invest other people's money in larger amounts, usually when the company is growing and needs a boost to scale up rapidly.

How to Approach Venture Capitalists

Approaching VCs is a strategic process. Make sure your business is in a phase where it can demonstrate potential for high growth and strong returns. Document your business model, growth strategy, competitive analysis, and financial forecast in a convincing investor pitch deck.

Venture capitalists appreciate founders who have done thorough market research, so ensure that you seem knowledgeable about the industry and your competitors. Understand that VCs are looking for firms that can give a substantial return on investment, typically within 5-7 years.

How to Approach Angel Investors

Similar to VCs, angel investors also require a well-structured business strategy. However, since angel investors invest at a much earlier stage and take on higher risks, they have a more in-depth focus on the founding team. They need faith in your passion, commitment, and capabilities as much as in the business concept. A warm introduction, possibly from a mutual connection, often works best when reaching out to angel investors.

Post-Funding Relationships

After securing funding, it's crucial to maintain an excellent working relationship with your VC or angel investor. Regular communication and transparency about business progress are key. Keep them updated about key decisions, achievements, and challenges. Also, leverage their expertise, network, and mentorship to facilitate growth.

5.3 Navigating the Fundraising Process

Securing funding for your tech startup can be a daunting process, especially for first-time entrepreneurs. This guide will provide you with valuable insights and strategies for navigating the complex world of fundraising and securing the requisite financial resources for your startup.

Step 1: Evaluate Your Funding Needs

Before embarking on the fundraising journey, you should determine how much funding your tech startup requires to achieve its goals. This includes considering the costs for product development, marketing, and operations. Creating a detailed financial plan will help you understand your funding requirements and assist you in presenting a strong case to potential investors.

Step 2: Understand Your Funding Options

Explore and understand the various funding options available for your startup, such as:

- Bootstrapping: Self-financing your startup by utilizing your personal savings, credit cards, or getting help from friends and family.

- Crowdfunding: Raising funds from numerous individuals through online platforms such as Kickstarter or Indiegogo.

- Angel Investors: Wealthy individuals who invest in early-stage startups in exchange for equity or debt.

- Venture Capital: Firms that invest in high-growth startups in exchange for equity and often provide mentorship and industry connections.

- Grants and Loans: Government or private organizations offering funding support to startups, typically in the form of non-dilutive funding, competitions, or loans.

Choose the type of funding that aligns best with your needs, strategy, and values.

Step 3: Develop a Powerful Pitch

A convincing pitch is essential for attracting potential investors. To create a remarkable pitch, focus on:

- Demonstrating the problem you are solving and why your solution is a better fit compared to existing products/services.
- Introduce your team, highlighting your experience and expertise relevant to your industry.
- Present a coherent business plan, including product development, go-to-market strategy, financial projections, and growth potential.
- Explain how much funding you need and how you plan to utilize it to scale your business.

Step 4: Network and Establish Connections

Building a strong network is crucial for fundraising success. Start by:

- Attending industry events, conferences, and meetups to establish connections with potential investors.
- Joining online forums, LinkedIn groups, and other relevant communities for your industry.
- Asking for introductions by colleagues or mentors who have connections with potential investors.

Step 5: Engage and Pitch to Investors

Once you have identified potential investors that align with your business, reach out to them with a tailored approach. Be professional, concise, and respectful of their time. Send them a brief introductory email, explaining your business and attaching relevant documents like your pitch deck. If they show interest, follow up with a more detailed conversation and schedule a meeting to present your pitch.

Step 6: Due Diligence and Closing the Deal

After a successful pitch, investors often perform due diligence, which typically involves reviewing your financials, legal documents, team background, and market opportunity. Ensure your documentation is in order and transparent. After favorable due diligence results, negotiate the terms, and sign the necessary agreements to secure your funding.

Chapter six

Product Development and Design

6.1 Creating a Minimum Viable Product (MVP)

An essential step for modern tech startups is the creation of a Minimum Viable Product (MVP) during their product development and design phase. The MVP is a crucial tool that allows startups to gauge their target audience's interest in their product, gather valuable feedback, and iterate quickly to refine their product offerings. In this guide, we will share pivotal insights and practical steps to help tech innovators develop a rewarding MVP.

Step 1: Identify and Understand Your Target Market

Gaining insight into your target market is the foundation upon which you will build your MVP. Conduct market research and interviews with potential customers to understand their needs, pain points, and expectations. Focusing on a specific niche or target audience will provide you with the opportunity to address their specific concerns in your MVP, increasing its relevance and impact.

Step 2: Define the Problem and Value Proposition

Once you thoroughly understand your target market, define the primary problem your product aims to solve. The perceived value of your product relies on a clear understanding of the problem you are addressing. State your value proposition concisely, ensuring it communicates the unique benefits and solutions your product provides in comparison to competitors.

Step 3: Outline Your Product's Core Features

Rather than overwhelming your MVP with multiple features, focus on the core features necessary to solve the identified problem. To do so:

- List all potential features for your product.
- Prioritize these features based on their importance to the problem solution and your value proposition.
- Determine which features are essential for the MVP and which can be added in future iterations.

Remember, the goal of your MVP is to validate your product concept and receive feedback to make informed decisions about future features and enhancements.

Step 4: Design and Develop Your MVP

Once you have identified the core features, initiate your MVP's design and development. Collaborate with your product development team or external partners for tasks such as wireframing, prototyping, and coding. Focus on creating a user interface (UI) that is visually appealing, easy to understand, and enhances the user experience (UX) to encourage engagement.

Utilize agile development methodologies, such as Scrum or Kanban, to ensure rapid iteration, flexibility, and adaptability throughout the development process.

Step 5: Test and Validate Your MVP

Before releasing your MVP to early adopters, conduct thorough testing to identify and fix any issues, ensuring it meets the desired quality standards. Testing should involve:

- Unit tests: Assess individual components of the product for functionality.
- Integration tests: Ensure the interoperability of different components.

- Usability tests: Examine the product from a user's perspective to identify UX issues and areas for improvement.

- Once your MVP is optimized, launch it for a select group of early adopters to gather their valuable feedback and insights.

Step 6: Gather Feedback and Iterate

The release of your MVP marks the beginning of a continuous feedback loop essential for informed decision-making and growth. Listen to feedback from early users and analyze data collected during the MVP usage to identify improvements or new feature opportunities. Based on this feedback, make necessary changes and continue iterating until you have a refined product ready for widespread release.

6.2 Implementing an iterative development process

An iterative development process, which involves repeated cycles of designing, developing, testing, and revising, is vital for modern tech innovators. It allows room for continuous improvement, adapts to changes quickly, and reduces costly mistakes during product development. This guide will provide you with a comprehensive roadmap for implementing an iterative process in your startup, ensuring your product accurately serves its intended users.

Step 1: Define Your Project Scope and Goals

Begin by clearly defining the scope of your project and the goals you aim to achieve with your product. This includes understanding your target users, their needs, the problem your product is trying to solve, and the key features required. A well-defined project scope effectively guides your product development team and sets a clear vision for your product.

Step 2: Break Down Tasks

Based on your project scope and defined goals, break down your development tasks into small, manageable chunks. This process, often referred to as backlog refinement or grooming, helps ensure each task is well-understood, estimated, and ready for the team to start work upon.

Step 3: The Iterative Cycle

Iterative development revolves around short development cycles, or "iterations", where each cycle involves planning, designing, coding, and testing phases. The iteration ends with a review and retrospective to identify what went well, what challenges were encountered, and what improvements can be made.

1. Plan

   Establish what tasks are to be completed in the upcoming iteration based on your product backlog and team capacity.

2. Design

   Design the features or elements set out in your plan, focusing on usability and positive user experience.

3. Code

   This is the phase where your designs come to life. Developers code the software based on the defined designs and functional requirements.

4. Test

   Carry out systematic tests, such as unit testing, integration testing, and usability testing, to check for bugs, system errors, and user experience.

5. Review & Retrospective

   Once testing is complete, review the functionality of the iteration's work. Seek feedback from stakeholders to understand if it meets their expectations and take notes on areas for improvement, to be applied in the next iteration.

Step 4: Involve Stakeholders and Users

It's crucial to involve stakeholders (internal team, clients, investors) and users in the iterative process. Offering product demos and prototypes to stakeholders and getting early user feedback ensures that you're on track and meeting expectations. It helps prevent any costly surprise changes in the latter stages of the project.

Step 5: Documentation

Maintain clear and consistent documentation throughout your iterative process. This includes recording project requirements, design specifications, user feedback, testing results, and any changes made during each iteration. Good documentation ensures everyone on the team stays informed and helps achieve smoother handovers and transitions throughout the project.

Step 6: Learn, Adapt and Iterate Until Completion

Iterative development is an ongoing learning process. After each iteration, take feedback, learn from the experience, and adapt your plans for the next cycle. Continually reassess and adjust until your end product fits the intended purpose and meets the requirements.

6.3 Incorporating User Feedback into the Product Design

Understanding and integrating user feedback into the product design process is a powerful approach for tech innovators. It places the customer's needs and experiences at the heart of the design process, ensuring the product genuinely addresses user needs and performs optimally. Let's delve into how your startup can effectively incorporate user feedback into the product design phase.

Step 1: Gather User Feedback

The first step is to gather user feedback, which requires diverse and various strategies to ensure a comprehensive understanding of your users' experiences. Some effective methods include:

- User Interviews: Speak to users directly and ask them about their experiences, feelings, and suggestions regarding your product.
- Surveys: Use online tools to send out surveys asking specific questions about elements of your product.

- Usability Testing: Have users execute tasks on your platform and observe their interactions and issues.

- Feedback Boxes/Forms: Allow users to give their suggestions or report issues in real-time as they use the product.

- Social Media Listening: Monitor social media platforms for any mentions or discussions about your product.

Step 2: Analyze the Feedback

Once you have gathered feedback, it's important to perform a comprehensive analysis. Look for patterns, recurring themes, and shared experiences among your users. It's also helpful to categorize feedback, separating technical glitches from suggestions for new features or changes.

Step 3: Prioritize Changes Based on Feedback

Post-analysis, you'll be faced with a list of potential changes. Prioritize these changes according to their overall impact on user experience and your business objectives. A useful framework to employ here is the "Impact vs. Effort Matrix." This matrix will help you quickly identify changes that are low effort but offer high impact, prioritizing these over changes that are high effort but low impact.

Step 4: Design and Develop Changes

With an understanding of what needs to be changed, you can start incorporating the feedback into the design. Prototype these changes and involve your development team to create a realistic representation of the new design.

Step 5: Test New Features

Before rolling out changes to all users, test new features or designs thoroughly. This can be achieved through A/B testing or by releasing the new version to a subset of users. Gather feedback specifically about the new changes to determine if they've addressed the previously identified issues or areas for improvement.

Step 6: Release and Monitor the Implementation

Finally, release the adjustments to your entire user base and closely monitor user experience and product performance. Look out for feedback indicating whether the changes have positively impacted users. Always be ready for further iteration; the process of improvement is ongoing.

Chapter seven

Intellectual Property Protection

7.1 Importance of protecting intellectual property rights

Intellectual Property (IP) is a crucial asset for tech innovators, and its protection is not just a legal necessity but a strategic move for business growth. In this section, we will explore the importance of protecting intellectual property rights, its benefits, and the role it plays in safeguarding and enhancing business value for tech startups.

Why Protect Intellectual Property Rights?

Intellectual property allows tech innovators to claim ownership over their creations, shielding them from usage without permission and granting them exclusive rights to produce, sell, and profit from their innovations. Let's examine the top reasons why IP protection is crucial for tech startups.

1. Cultivating a Competitive Advantage

    Having a unique, groundbreaking idea gives startups an initial edge, but it's the protection of that idea through IP rights that ensures a sustained competitive advantage. IP protection prevents competitors from copying your idea or creating similar products, maintaining your market exclusivity.

2. Enhancing Business Value

> IP rights can increase the value of your startup. Patents, trademarks, and copyrights can be sold, licensed, or used as collateral for loans, providing startups with new revenue opportunities. Investors and venture capitalists often look at a startup's IP portfolio when considering investments as it often hints towards the potential for a high return on investment.

3. Boosting Startup Reputation and Confidence

> IP rights can build a startup's reputation by showcasing creativity, innovation, and forethought. It possibly indicates that the business understands its intellectual assets' worth and has made strategic moves to

safeguard them. This fosters confidence among stakeholders, including partners, investors, and customers.

4. Preventing Litigation

It's essential to secure IP rights for your startup to avoid future legal disputes. If another company has, unknowingly or otherwise, infringed upon your IP, having the appropriate legal protections in place allows you to defend your business and possibly receive compensation if your rights are violated.

Types of Intellectual Property Protections

Different kinds of IP protections exist for diverse forms of intellectual assets. Here are the most common ones tech startups should consider:

1. Patents

   A patent protects an invention, giving the patent owner exclusive rights to make, use, sell, or import the invention for a specific period, often 20 years. It is especially crucial for product-based tech startups that have developed new technologies.

2. Copyrights

   Copyright protection applies to original works of authorship, such as code, website content, marketing materials, and software products. It allows the holder to control reproduction, distribution, public performance, and public display of the copyrighted work.

3. Trademarks

   Trademarks protect logos, names, and designs associated with your brand, which distinguishes your startup's products or services from competitors.

4. Trade Secrets

   Trade secrets include confidential information that provides a business with a competitive edge, like certain algorithms, methods, or tactics. They are protected as long as they remain secret and confer some sort of economic benefit on its holder.

7.2 Handling IP disputes and infringement issues

Intellectual Property (IP) disputes and infringement issues are a looming threat for tech startups navigating a competitive marketplace. Handling these issues requires tact, strategic understanding, and a proactive approach to enforce and protect your IP rights. Here is a comprehensive guide on managing IP disputes and infringement scenarios, ensuring your startup continues its upward trajectory unimpeded.

Identifying Infringement

Identifying infringement is the first step towards resolving IP disputes. Regularly monitor the market and the activities of competitor companies to spot any unauthorized usage of your IP. For patents, this means identifying products that use your patented invention. For trademarks, this involves spotting similar or identical names, logos, or designs that could potentially confuse customers. For copyright, it will be any unauthorized use of your original works.

Seek Legal Advice

Once you've identified a potential infringement, the next move is to seek legal counsel. An IP attorney can guide you on the best course of action considering the evidence at hand, the risk associated with the infringement, and the potential costs and benefits involved.

Cease and Desist Notice

A common first step is to send a cease-and-desist letter to the infringing party. This formal correspondence asserts your rights, outlines the infringement, and demands that the infringing activities stop. Ensure that this action doesn't escalate the situation unnecessarily, as sometimes a diplomatic, informal approach can be more effective.

Negotiations and Licensing

Another alternative to litigation is negotiations. You can work with the infringing party to reach a settlement or license agreement. Licensing could turn an infringement issue into a new revenue stream, as it allows others to use your IP rights in return for payment.

Alternative Dispute Resolution

Alternative Dispute Resolution (ADR) methods such as mediation and arbitration are also viable options to resolve IP disputes with less cost and time than formal litigation. ADR provides a venue for both parties to discuss their interests and concerns, often leading to a mutually agreeable outcome.

Litigation

If all else fails, litigation may be necessary. Litigating an IP infringement dispute generally requires evidence of the infringement, an assessment of the damages incurred, and a determination of whether these damages can be recovered.

However, litigation should be a last resort, considering the potential costs, the time involved, and the risk of a negative outcome. A legal counsel can provide guidance on whether pursuing litigation would be strategically beneficial.

Preventing IP Disputes

Prevention is the best way to handle IP disputes and infringement issues. This includes:

- Robust IP Protection: Ensure your patents, trademarks, or copyrights are in place, covering all jurisdictions where your product is being sold or used.

- Regular Monitoring: Regularly monitor the market and competitors. Early detection of potential infringement gives more options to handle the situation before it escalates.

- Education and Awareness: Foster an understanding of IP rights within your team. The more aware they are of infringement issues, the better they can prevent any unauthorized usage of your IP.

7.3 Obtaining patents, trademarks, and copyrights

Securing Intellectual Property (IP) rights for your tech startup's inventions, brands, and original works is a critical component of establishing a successful business. Acquiring patents, trademarks, and copyrights is essential for safeguarding your competitive advantage and fostering long-term growth. In this guide, we will explore the process of obtaining these key IP protections.

Patents

Patents provide legal protection for inventions, giving the patent owner the exclusive right to use, manufacture, and sell a product or process for a specified period, usually 20 years. Here is an outline of the patent application process:

1. Assess Patentability

Before filing your patent application, assess whether your invention is eligible for patent protection. The main criteria include:

- Novelty: The invention must be new and not previously disclosed in any other sources.
- Non-Obviousness: The invention must not be an obvious extension of existing information or technology.
- Usefulness: The invention must have a practical applicability and serve a useful purpose.

2. Conduct a Prior Art Search

A thorough Prior Art Search is required to ensure your invention doesn't infringe on any existing patents and identify related patents that can affect your application process.

3. Prepare and File a Patent Application

Once you've assessed the patentability of your invention and conducted a Prior Art Search, prepare your patent application. This involves:

- A detailed description of your invention, including its technical specifications, methodology, and any drawings or diagrams.

- Clearly defined claims outlining the scope of your invention and what you wish to protect.

- An abstract summarizing your invention in a concise manner.

You can file your application with the appropriate national or regional patent office, such as the United States Patent and Trademark Office (USPTO) in the U.S. or the European Patent Office (EPO) in the European Union.

4. Examination and Prosecution

The patent office will review your application to determine if your invention meets the patentability requirements. You may be required to communicate with the patent examiner and respond to any objections or questions.

5. Patent Issuance or Rejection

Once your application is examined and approved, the patent office will issue your patent, granting you legal protection for your invention. If your application is rejected, you may have the option to appeal the decision or address the issues.

Trademarks

Trademarks protect names, logos, symbols, or slogans that identify and distinguish a brand. The process for obtaining a trademark includes the following steps:

1. Choose a Distinctive Mark

Create a mark that is unique, easily recognizable, and not too similar to existing trademarks within your industry.

2. Conduct a Trademark Search

Research existing trademarks using online databases, such as the USPTO's Trademark Electronic Search System (TESS), to ensure there are no conflicts with your chosen mark.

3. File a Trademark Application

After confirming your desired mark is available, file the trademark application with the appropriate national trademark office.

4. Monitor and Respond to Examination Process

The trademark office will review your application and may require further clarification or amendments. Respond to any correspondence promptly and accurately.

5. Trademark Registration

If approved, your trademark will be published in the trademark register, granting you legal protection.

Copyrights

Copyrights protect original works of authorship, including literary, musical, and artistic works. Here's a brief overview of how to obtain copyright protection:

1. Create an Original Work

Ensure that your work is original and not derived from someone else's creation.

2. Register Your Work

In countries like the U.S., you can register your copyright with the appropriate government office, such as the U.S. Copyright Office. Registration is not mandatory but provides legal benefits in case of a dispute.

3. Mark Your Work

Although not required, placing a copyright notice (e.g., © Year of Creation, Your Name) on your work indicates that you claim ownership, deterring potential infringement.

Conclusion

Building a tech startup from scratch is a daunting yet thrilling venture. This Start-Up Guide for Tech Innovators serves as your compass, navigating the myriad of entrepreneurial trials and tribulations. It ushered you into the realm of ideation and market research and highlighted the importance of building a competent team. It further illuminated nuances of fundraising strategies, product development, and market penetration tactics.

An undercurrent throughout this journey is the crucial role of Intellectual Property Protection. Patents, trademarks, and copyrights can be your guiding beacon amidst a sea of competition, securing your startup's unique identity, insulating it against infringements, and providing a springboard for long-term growth. As you delve into handling IP disputes and infringement issues, you learn that the fine art of conflict resolution and preventive measures is just as important as obtaining IP rights.

Obtaining patents, trademarks, and copyrights provides your startup with a protective aegis. Beyond legal defense, they become your startup's unique identifiers, contributing to your business's overall reputation and market value.

In conclusion, launching a tech startup is more than a mere amalgamation of resources or ideas – it is an orchestrated execution of a vision, an amalgamation of leadership acumen, market sensibility, technological insight, and decisive strategies.

As a tech innovator, you are poised at the brink of a path of incredible possibilities. Remember, every successful startup is built on passion and resilience. Approach every challenge as an opportunity to learn and grow, extend your horizons, and let innovation be your guiding force. Stay adaptable, keep learning, embrace change, and venture forth to imprint your indelible mark in the world of technology. Welcome to the exhilarating entrepreneurial journey!

www.ingramcontent.com/pod-product-compliance
Lightning Source LLC
Chambersburg PA
CBHW071256050326
40690CB00011B/2426